Learn to Read Arabic in 5 Days

YOUSSEF FAHMY

Published by Wolfedale Press 2016

WOLFEDALE PRESS

Cover image by Nadine Doerle

ISBN: 978-1532765285

CONTENTS

Introduction	i
Unit 1 – ب, ك, م, د	1
Unit 2 – ا, س, ت, ن	3
Unit 3 – ش, ر, ل, ي	7
Unit 4 – ج, و, ة	11
Unit 5 – خ, ف, ز, ه	13
Unit 6 – ث, غ, ق	15
Unit 7 – ذ, ح, ع	17
Unit 8 – ء, لا	21
Unit 9 – ص, ض, ط, ظ	23
Unit 10 – Review	25
Appendix – Short Vowels and Diacritics	27
Arabic Alphabet	29
Glossary – Thematic Order	31
Glossary – Alphabetical Order	39

INTRODUCTION

Learning a new alphabet can be very intimidating for an English speaker only used to reading the Latin alphabet. This is partly why English speakers tend to stick to learning other languages that use the same alphabet, such as French, Spanish and Italian – because they seem a lot easier!

But learning a new alphabet does not have to be so difficult. The difficulty is finding a good system to learn the new alphabet so that the student does not get discouraged and give up before making any real progress. Making progress in the language is the best motivator.

The secret to learning a new alphabet is to be taught each letter separately, and then to practice how the new letters combine with letters you already know to read real words in the language in a structured way. This is not revolutionary – it is probably how you learned to read English – but it is not easy to find for other languages.

This book will teach you how to read the Arabic alphabet in exactly that way, and with this method you will be able to read Arabic in only 5 days or less! After that you will be able to enjoy the Arabic language and culture in a way that you were never able to before

THE ARABIC ALPHABET
الأبجدية العربية

The Arabic alphabet contains 28 letters and is written from right to left, the opposite direction of English. The Arabic alphabet does not contain different upper and lowercase letters, however, the Arabic alphabet is exclusively written cursively. This means that letters slightly change shape in order to connect to the previous and following letters in a word, similar to English cursive handwriting. This cursive character is always maintained, even on computers; when one types letters in the Arabic alphabet, the software joins the letters together. Letters are never allowed to be left unconnected.

Vowels are not usually written in Arabic, although some consonants are used to represent long vowels. A system does exist to fully spell out the short vowels as a series of dashes and lines above and below the word. The vowel markings are only used in certain texts, however, such as religious texts and books for children, and are not seen in most publications. The vowel symbols are included in an appendix in this book, however they are not included in the main lesson units because it is important to get used to reading without them.

The lack of written vowels makes the Arabic alphabet somewhat challenging for beginners, since it is not always clear exactly how to pronounce a word one sees written. However, much like Modern English with its weird spellings, once you develop a feel for the language, it is actually not at all as difficult as it seems at first. There is a definite pattern to Arabic words and after some practice it is usually obvious how a word should be pronounced – even without the vowels.

HOW TO USE THIS COURSE

The primary goal of this course book is to teach the reader to recognize the Arabic alphabet and to begin to read the Arabic language.

The main way this is accomplished is by teaching the individual pronunciations of each letter, and then utilizing "Practice" sections where the student can practice reading real Arabic words. These "Practice" sections are very important and the main way the student will start to feel comfortable with the Arabic alphabet. The answers to all "Practice" questions are included directly below the questions, but try to avoid looking at the answers until you have attempted to answer the questions yourself.

Throughout the book, the reader will also learn approximately 150 real Arabic words. These words have been carefully selected to be of maximum benefit to beginner students of the language and are a great starting point for students who want to continue their study of Arabic. In the end of the book there are two glossaries – one in thematic order and one in alphabetical order – where the student can study and memorize all the words learned in this course.

The course material has been designed to be completed slowly over five days, while reviewing lessons as necessary. You are encouraged to go at whatever pace you feel comfortable with and to feel free to go back to lessons to review as much as needed.

Good luck and I hope you enjoy the first step on your journey to learning the Arabic language.

UNIT 1 - ب, ك, م, د

The first letter introduced in this course is the Arabic letter ب. This letter is pronounced like the "b" sound in "boy" (IPA: /b/). Arabic is a cursive script and most letters change shape slightly in order to join to the surrounding letters. The letter ب has four different forms, isolated, initial, medial and final, depending on its place in the word; these forms are (from right to left):

ب بـ ـبـ ـب

Note that although the shape of the letter changes, the single dot below the letter stays the same. These dots are crucial in Arabic and the main way to distinguish letters.

The letter ك is pronounced like the "k" sound in "kite" (IPA: /k/). Like ب, ك changes shape depending on its place in the word. The isolated, initial, medial and final forms are:

ك كـ ـكـ ـك

Notice that only the initial and final forms have the extra "s" shaped stroke in the letter. This extra detail is often left out in handwriting but is always present in formal printed documents.

The letter م is pronounced like the English "m" in "mother" or "Mary" (IPA: /m/). Like the two letters above, م has four forms:

م مـ ـمـ ـم

The last letter of this unit is the letter د, which is pronounced like the English "d" sound in "dad" (IPA: /d/).

There are two types of letters in Arabic with respect to how they join with other letters. The first three letters in the unit, ب, ك, and م have four different forms because they join to the previous and following letters.

The other type has only two forms because it never joins to the letter that follows it. The letter د is the second type. The two forms of this letter (isolated and final) are:

د ـد

PRACTICE

Try to recognize these English words in their Arabic disguises. Remember that Arabic is written from right to left and short vowels are not written. The answers are below.

1. بد
2. بك
3. دب
4. دم
5. مد
6. دك

ANSWERS

1. bad (or bed)
2. back
3. dab
4. dam
5. mad
6. deck

UNIT 2 - ا, س, ت, ن

When a word begins with a vowel sound in Arabic, that vowel is written with a ا regardless of the vowel. There are three vowel sounds in Arabic, "a", "i" and "u", and all three vowels have long and short versions. It is usually helpful to assume that ا is a long "a" sound, but it can actually be any of the three vowels at the beginning of a word.

When the letter ا is written in the middle or the end of a word it is always a long "a" sound like the "a" sound in "father" (IPA /a:/). Long vowels will be written in this book with a bar or macron above the vowel, e.g. ā. Long vowels are always stressed in Arabic and are held for longer than short vowels. Remember that short vowels are not written in Arabic. The letter ا has only two forms since it can only connect to the previous letter. Those two forms are:

ا ـا

The Arabic letter س is pronounced like the "s" sound in "some" (IPA: /s/). س connects to the previous and the following letters, and therefore has four different forms:

س سـ ـسـ ـس

The letter ت is pronounced like the "t" sound in "ten" or "Tom" (IPA: /t/). ت has the following four forms depending on its position in the word:

ت تـ ـتـ ـت

The letter ن is pronounced like the "n" sound in "now" (IPA: /n/). ن has the following four forms depending on its position in the word:

ن نـ ـنـ ـن

TRY NOT TO CONFUSE

The letters ب, ت, and ن have the same basic shape in all of their forms and are therefore distinguished only by the number and position of their dots. Remember that ب has one dot under the line and is pronounced "b", ت has two dots above the line and is pronounced "t" and ن has one dot above the line and is pronounced "n". Always pay close attention to the dots when reading Arabic.

PRACTICE 1

Try to recognize these English words in their Arabic disguises. Focus on the approximate pronunciation and not necessarily the English spelling. Remember the short and long "a" sounds. The answers are below.

1. كن
2. كت
3. كتس
4. مت
5. انت
6. بت
7. بات
8. تنك

ANSWERS 1

1. can
2. cat
3. cats
4. mat
5. ant (or aunt)
6. bat (short "a" sound)
7. bought (long "a" sound)
8. tank

PRACTICE 2

Now try to read these real Arabic words. The English translation is given next to each word. The correct pronunciations are given in the answers below.

1. دم	(blood)
2. بنت	(daughter / girl)
3. بنك	(bank)
4. باب	(door)
5. كتاب	(book)
6. بدن	(body)

ANSWERS 2

1. dam
2. bint
3. bank
4. bāb
5. kitāb
6. badan

UNIT 3 - ش, ر, ل, ي

The Arabic letter ش is pronounced like the "sh" sound in "she" (IPA: /ʃ/). Although written with two letters in English, "sh" is really one sound and it is written with a single letter in Arabic. The "sh" pronunciation will be represented by š in this book. Like س, ش connects to the previous and the following letters, and therefore has four different forms:

ش شـ ـشـ ـش

The letter ر is pronounced with an "r" sound (IPA: /r/). The "r" sound is similar to the trilled or rolled "r" sound in the Spanish "perro", but English speakers can use the English "r" sound in "rope" and be understood. ر only connects to the previous letter and has only two forms:

ر ـر

The letter ل is pronounced like the "l" sound in "like" (IPA: /l/). ل connects to the previous and the following letters, and therefore has four different forms:

ل لـ ـلـ ـل

The letter ي is pronounced like the "y" sound in "yellow" when used at the beginning of a word (IPA: /j/). When used in the middle or end of a word, ي is either pronounced with a long vowel sound like the "ee" in "bee" (IPA: /iː/), or like the "y" in "bay". When ي is pronounced "ee", this will be represented by ī in the pronunciation in this book, otherwise as a "y". ي connects to the previous and the following letters, and therefore has four different forms:

ي يـ ـيـ ـي

TRY NOT TO CONFUSE

The letters ا, and ل can be easy to confuse as they both consist of straight vertical lines. The main difference between these two letters is that ا does not connect to the following letter, and ل does.

In its initial and medial forms ـيـ resembles ـبـ, ـتـ and ـنـ. As always pay close attention to the number and position of the dots in order to differentiate these letters.

PRACTICE

Try to read these real Arabic words. The English translation is given next to each word. The correct pronunciations are given in the answers below.

1. كلب	(dog)
2. بيت	(house)
3. بلد	(country / state)
4. كرسي	(chair)
5. شاي	(tea)
6. شمس	(sun)
7. نار	(fire)
8. كبير	(big)
9. بارد	(cold)
10. مسلم	(Muslim)
11. يناير	(January)
12. مارس	(March)

ANSWERS

1. kalb
2. bayt
3. balad
4. kursī
5. šāy
6. šams
7. nār
8. kabīr
9. bārid
10. muslim
11. yanāyīr
12. mars

UNIT 4 - ج, و, ة

The letter ج is pronounced like the "j" sound in "jam" (IPA: /dʒ/). ج connects to the previous and following letters and has the four following forms:

ج جـ ـجـ ـج

When written at the beginning of a word, the letter و is pronounced like the "w" in "we" (IPA: /w/). After a consonant, و is pronounced with a long "oo" sound (IPA: /u/), and after another vowel like the "w" sound in "now". When و is pronounced "oo", this will be represented by ū in the pronunciation in this book, otherwise as a "w". و only connects to the preceding letter and not the following letter and so has the following two forms:

و ـو

The letter ة is technically not a separate letter but actually a special form of the letter ت (notice the two dots above the letter). This form is only written at the end of a word and is pronounced with an "a" sound. Since this form is only ever written at the end of the word, if anything else is added to the word, such as a grammatical ending, the ة changes to a regular ت and pronounced with a "t" sound. Since ة is only used at the end of a word, it only has two forms:

ة ـة

PRACTICE

Try to read these Arabic words. The English translation is given next to each word. The correct pronunciations are given in the answers below.

1. جبل	(mountain)
2. جليد	(ice)
3. مدينة	(city)
4. مسجد	(mosque)
5. ولد	(boy)
6. مدرسة	(school)
7. يوم	(day)
8. لون	(color)
9. سمكة	(fish)
10. شجرة	(tree)

ANSWERS

1. jabal
2. jalīd
3. madīna
4. masjid
5. walad
6. madrasa
7. yawm
8. lawn
9. samaka
10. šajara

UNIT 5 - خ, ف, ز, ه

The pronunciation of the Arabic letter خ does not exist in English. It is the "ch" sound in the German "doch" or the "j" sound in the Spanish "ojos" (IPA: /x/). It is a heavy throat clearing "h" sound. This letter will be represented as "kh" in the pronunciation in this book. خ connects to the previous and the following letters, and therefore has four different forms:

خ خـ ـخـ ـخ

The letter ف is pronounced like the "f" sound in "far" (IPA: /f/). ف connects to the previous and the following letters, and therefore has four different forms:

ف فـ ـفـ ـف

The letter ز is pronounced like the "z" sound in "zoo" (IPA: /z/). ز only connects to the previous letter and not the following letter and therefore has the following two forms:

ز ـز

The letter ه is pronounced like the "h" sound in "house" (IPA: /h/). ه connects to the previous and the following letters, and has four different forms:

ه هـ ـهـ ـه

PRACTICE

Try to read these Arabic words. The English translation is given next to each word. The correct pronunciations are given in the answers below.

1. خبز	(bread)
2. خمسة	(five)
3. الخميس	(Thursday)
4. فم	(mouth)
5. زهرة	(flower)
6. شهر	(month)
7. نهر	(river)
8. فبراير	(February)

ANSWERS

1. khubz
2. khamsa
3. al-khamīs
4. fam
5. zahra
6. šahr
7. nahr
8. fibrāyīr

UNIT 6 - ث, غ, ق

The letter ث is pronounced like the "th" sound in "thin" (IPA: /θ/). ث connects to the previous and the following letters, and therefore has four different forms:

ث ثـ ـثـ ـث

The pronunciation of the Arabic letter غ does not exist in English (IPA: /ɣ/). It is similar to a "g" sound but pronounced further back in the throat giving it a more guttural sound. If you know French it is pretty similar to the French "r" sound in words like "rue". This letter will be represented as "gh" in the pronunciation in this book. غ connects to the previous and the following letters, and therefore has four different forms:

غ غـ ـغـ ـغ

The letter ق is pronounced with another sound not present in English. It is similar to the "k" sound in "cut" but pronounced further back in the throat (IPA: /q/). This sound will be represented by q in this book. ق connects to the previous and the following letters, and therefore has the following four forms:

ق قـ ـقـ ـق

Unfortunately for an English speaker, Arabic pronunciation is difficult as there are several sounds that do not exist in English and a few that do not exist in any European language. The goal of this book is to teach you to recognize the letters and read the Arabic language, and I would highly recommend working with a native speaker on the pronunciation of the difficult letters after you have mastered the alphabet.

PRACTICE

Try to read these Arabic words. The English translation is given next to each word. The correct pronunciations are given in the answers below.

1. اثنان	(two)
2. ثمانية	(eight)
3. القاهرة	(Cairo)
4. بقرة	(cow)
5. قارب	(January)
6. فندق	(hotel)
7. سوق	(market)
8. غدا	(tomorrow)

ANSWERS

1. ithnān
2. thamāniya
3. al-qāhira
4. baqara
5. qārib
6. funduq
7. suq
8. ghadan (final "n" not shown in writing)

UNIT 7 - ذ, ح, ع

The Arabic letter ذ is pronounced like the "th" sound in "then" (IPA: /ð/). Notice that although they are both written "th" in English, this is not the same sound as the "th" in "thin". This letter will be represented by "dh" in the pronunciation sections of this book. ذ connects to the previous letter but not the following letter and has therefore has only two forms:

ذ ـذ

The pronunciation of the letter ح does not exist in English. It is like an "h" sound but more heavy and articulated further back in the throat. It sounds a little like blowing warm air on your cold hands (IPA: /ħ/). This letter will be represented by ḥ in this book (an "h" with a dot below). ح connects to the previous and the following letters, and has four different forms:

ح حـ ـحـ ـح

The letter ع is difficult to pronounce and sometimes even difficult to hear. It is a consonant that is pronounced so far back in the throat that you use the same muscles as you use when gagging (IPA: /ʕ/). This is not a common sound in other language in the world but is very prevalent in Arabic. Since there is no good way to write this sound in English, I will be using the Arabic letter to represent this sound even in the transcription. ع connects to the previous and the following letters, and has the following four forms:

ع عـ ـعـ ـع

TRY NOT TO CONFUSE

As we have seen, many letters in Arabic have the same shapes and are only distinguished by the number and placement of the dots. It is therefore very important to always pay close attention to the dots when reading Arabic.

To review, study the letters below; the letters with the same shapes have been grouped together with their pronunciations shown below the letter.

ـبـ	ـتـ	ـثـ	ـنـ	ـيـ
b	t	th	n	y / ī

ـجـ	ـحـ	ـخـ
j	ḥ	kh

ـد	ـذ
d	dh
ـر	ـز
r	z
ـسـ	ـشـ
s	š
ـعـ	ـغـ
ع	gh
ـفـ	ـقـ
f	q

PRACTICE

Try to read these Arabic words. The English translation is given next to each word. The correct pronunciations are given in the answers below.

1. نافذة	(window)
2. ذراع	(arm)
3. لحم	(meat)
4. لحية	(beard)
5. نعم	(yes)
6. عين	(eye)
7. حزين	(sad)
8. سعيد	(happy)
9. ساعة	(hour)
10. بحر	(sea)
11. حليب	(milk)
12. عربي	(Arabic)

ANSWERS

1. nāfidha
2. dhirāع
3. laḥm
4. liḥya
5. naعam
6. عayn
7. ḥazīn
8. saعīd
9. sāعa
10. baḥr
11. ḥalīb
12. عarabī

UNIT 8 - ء, لا

The two symbols introduced in this unit are not technically letters of the Arabic alphabet, but are special symbols used in Arabic writing in addition to the regular 28 "full" letters of the alphabet.

The symbol ء, called hamza, is used to indicate a glottal stop (IPA: /ʔ/). A glottal stop is a catch in the throat or a slight pause between vowels, like in the word "uh-oh". This pronunciation will be shown as ' (single quotation mark) in this book. The hamza does not connect to other letters but is written "seated" on other letters. Some examples of how ء can be written are:

أ إ ئـ ـؤ ـئ ـاء

The full spelling rules for the hamza are complicated and outside the scope of this book, but one important thing to note is when a word begins with a hamza, it is written above the place-holding ا if followed by a short "a" or short "u" sound, and below the ا if followed by a short "i" sound.

A special ligature form is written when ل is followed by ا. This form does not change the pronunciation and is merely a special cursive form of the two letters. This special form connects to the previous letter but not to the following letter and has two forms:

لا ـلا

PRACTICE

Try to read these Arabic words. The English translation is given next to each word. The correct pronunciations are given in the answers below.

1. أحمر	(red)
2. أزرق	(blue)
3. لا	(no)
4. إسلام	(Islam)
5. ماء	(water)
6. عشاء	(dinner)
7. ثلاثة	(three)
8. الاثنين	(Monday)
9. سماء	(sky)

ANSWERS

1. 'aḥmar
2. 'azraq
3. lā
4. 'islām
5. mā'
6. ع ašā'
7. thalātha
8. al-ithnayn
9. samā'

UNIT 9 - ظ ,ط ,ض ,ص

The four letters introduced in this unit are known as the "emphatic" or strong consonants in Arabic. They are all pronounced in a similar way to another consonant but with the back of the tongue slightly raised and slightly more forcefully, or emphatically.

The letter ص is an "s" sound pronounced somewhat close to the "ss" in "massage" (IPA: /sˤ/). It is the emphatic version of س. All emphatic consonants will be represented in the pronunciation by a dot written below the similar sound, i.e. ṣ. ص connects to the previous and the following letters:

ص صـ ـصـ ـص

The letter ض is the emphatic counterpart of د. It is pronounced somewhat close to the "d" sound in "dark" (IPA: /dˤ/). It has the same four forms as ص and is distinguished by the single dot.

The letter ط is the emphatic counterpart of ت. It is pronounced somewhat similar to the "t" sound in "star" but more forcefully. (IPA: /tˤ/). ط connects to the previous and the following letters, and has the following four forms:

ط طـ ـطـ ـط

The letter ظ is the emphatic counterpart of ذ. It is therefore pronounced with a more forceful "th" sound like in "this" (IPA: /ðˤ/). Depending on the speaker, you may hear this letter pronounced as an emphatic "z" sound instead of "th". Following Arabic convention, this letter will be written ẓ in the pronunciation in this book. It has the same four forms as ط and is distinguished by the single dot.

PRACTICE

Try to read these Arabic words. The English translation is given next to each word. The correct pronunciations are given in the answers below.

1. صديق (friend)
2. حصان (horse)
3. أخضر (green)
4. طفل (child)
5. طائرة (airplane)
6. مطعم (restaurant)
7. عظم (bone)
8. قميص (shirt)
9. أصفر (yellow)
10. رمضان (Ramadan)

ANSWERS

1. ṣadīq
2. ḥiṣān
3. 'akhḍar
4. ṭifl
5. ṭā'ira
6. maṭعam
7. عaẓm
8. qamīṣ
9. 'aṣfar
10. ramaḍān

UNIT 10 - REVIEW

PRACTICE 1

Review the previous lessons by reading these real Arabic place names. The correct pronunciations are given in the Answers below.

1. الأردن
2. سوريا
3. أبو ظبي
4. قطر
5. لبنان
6. مصر
7. القاهرة
8. مكة
9. البحر الأحمر
10. المحيط الهندي

ANSWERS 1

1. al-'urdun (Jordan)
2. sūriyā (Syria)
3. 'abū ẓabī (Abu Dhabi)
4. qaṭar (Qatar)
5. lubnān (Lebanon)
6. miṣr (Egypt)
7. al-qāhira (Cairo)
8. makka (Mecca)
9. al-baḥr al-'aḥmar (The Red Sea)
10. al-muḥīṭ al-hindī (Indian Ocean)

PRACTICE 2

Review what you have learned in this book by reading the following Arabic names. The correct pronunciations are given in the Answers below.

1. محمد
2. حسن
3. حسين
4. إسماعيل
5. يوسف
6. عبدالله
7. علي
8. أحمد
9. عائشة
10. فاطمة

ANSWERS 2

1. Muḥammad
2. Ḥassan
3. Ḥusayn
4. 'Ismāعīl
5. Yūsuf
6. عabdu llāh
7. عalī
8. 'Aḥmad
9. عā'isha
10. Fāṭima

APPENDIX

SHORT VOWELS AND DIACRITICS

As we have learned, short vowels are not written in usual publications, such as newspapers, magazines, street signs and Arabic handwriting. There are occasional times when it is necessary to write the short vowels however, such as in books for children who are learning to read, or in the Qur'ān. The way these vowels are written is not through new letters, but by a series of diacritics written above and below the word.

The three short vowels may be written as follows:

The short "a" sound is written with a diagonal line placed above the letter, e.g.:

سَمَكَة

Which is pronounced "samaka".

The short "i" sound is written with a diagonal line placed below the letter, e.g.:

كِتَاب

Which is pronounced "kitab".

The short "u" sound is written with a small curl placed above the letter, e.g.:

فُطور

Which is pronounced "fuṭūr".

Apart from the short vowels there are a few more diacritics that are used in fully vocalized texts.

A small circle written above a consonant is used to mark the absence of a vowel, i.e. there is another consonant immediately afterwards, e.g.:

خُبْز

Which is pronounced "khubz".

A small shape with two loops that looks like a "w" is written above a consonant if that consonant is doubled. Doubled consonants are held longer than single consonants and are an important part of proper Arabic pronunciation. For example:

دُكَّان

Which is pronounced "dukkan".

Lastly, if one of the short vowel symbols is doubled at the end of a word, that signifies that there is an "n" sound after that vowel. For example:

غَدًا

The doubled diagonal above the د signifies that this word should be pronounced "ghadan".

These vowel symbols and extra diacritics are helpful to know. You will often see them written out in dictionaries to help learners know exactly how a word should be pronounced. Remember that they are normally not written, however, and to read Arabic successfully you need to get used to reading Arabic text without the use of any of these extra symbols.

ARABIC ALPHABET

Letter	Pronunciation
ا	[a], [i], [u]
ب	[b]
ت	[t]
ث	[th]
ج	[j]
ح	[ḥ]
خ	[kh]
د	[d]
ذ	[dh]
ر	[r]
ز	[z]
س	[s]
ش	[š]
ص	[ṣ]
ض	[ḍ]

ط	[ṭ]
ظ	[ẓ]
ع	[ع]
غ	[gh]
ف	[f]
ق	[q]
ک	[k]
ل	[l]
م	[m]
ن	[n]
ه	[h]
و	[w], [ū]
ی	[y], [ī]

GLOSSARY – THEMATIC ORDER

ANIMALS

حيوان	[ḥayawān]	animal
كلب	[kalb]	dog
قط	[qiṭṭ]	cat
سمكة	[samaka]	fish
طائر	[ṭā’ir]	bird
بقرة	[baqara]	cow
فأرة	[fa’ra]	mouse
حصان	[ḥiṣān]	horse
جمل	[jamal]	camel

PEOPLE

إنسان	[’insān]	person
أم	[’umm]	mother
أب	[’ab]	father
ابن	[ibn]	son
ولد	[walad]	boy
بنت	[bint]	daughter / girl
أخ	[’akh]	brother
أخت	[ukht]	sister
صديق	[ṣadīq]	friend
رجل	[rajul]	man
امرأة	[imra’a]	woman
طفل	[ṭifl]	child
رضيع	[raḍīع]	baby

TRANSPORTATION

قطار	[qiṭār]	train
طائرة	[ṭā'ira]	airplane
سيارة	[sayyāra]	car (automobile)
دراجة	[darrāja]	bicycle
باص	[bāṣ]	bus
قارب	[qārib]	boat

LOCATION

مدينة	[madīna]	city
بيت	[bayt]	house
شارع	[šāriع]	street
مطار	[maṭār]	airport
فندق	[funduq]	hotel
مطعم	[maṭعam]	restaurant
مدرسة	[madrasa]	school
جامعة	[jāmiعa]	university
حديقة	[ḥadīqa]	park
دكان	[dukkān]	store / shop
مستشفى	[mustašfa]	hospital
مسجد	[masjid]	mosque
كنيسة	[kanīsa]	church
بلد	[balad]	country (state)
بنك	[bank]	bank
سوق	[sūq]	market

HOME

طاولة	[ṭāwila]	table
كرسي	[kursī]	chair
نافذة	[nāfidha]	window
باب	[bāb]	door
كتاب	[kitāb]	book

CLOTHING

ملابس	[malābis]	clothing
قبعة	[qubbaعa]	hat
قميص	[qamīṣ]	shirt
بنطلون	[banṭalūn]	pants
حذاء	[ḥidhā']	shoe

BODY

بدن	[badan]	body
رأس	[ra's]	head
وجه	[wajh]	face
شعر	[šaعr]	hair
عين	[عayn]	eye
فم	[fam]	mouth
أنف	['anf]	nose
أذن	['udhun]	ear
ذراع	[dhirāع]	arm
رجل	[rijl]	leg / foot
يد	[yad]	hand
دم	[dam]	blood
عظم	[عaẓm]	bone
لحية	[liḥya]	beard

MISCELLANEOUS

نعم	[naƐam]	yes
لا	[lā]	no

FOOD & DRINK

طعام	[ṭaƐām]	food
لحم	[laḥm]	meat
خبز	[khubz]	bread
جبن	[jubn]	cheese
تفاحة	[tuffāḥa]	apple
ماء	[mā’]	water
بيرة	[bīra]	beer
عصير	[Ɛaṣīr]	juice
قهوة	[qahwa]	coffee
شاي	[šāy]	tea
حليب	[ḥalīb]	milk
فطور	[fuṭūr]	breakfast
غداء	[ghadā’]	lunch
عشاء	[Ɛašā’]	dinner

COLORS

لون	[lawn]	color
أحمر	[’aḥmar]	red
أزرق	[’azraq]	blue
أخضر	[’akhḍar]	green
أصفر	[’aṣfar]	yellow
أسود	[’aswad]	black
أبيض	[’abyaḍ]	white

NATURE

بحر	[baḥr]	sea
نهر	[nahr]	river
بحيرة	[buḥayra]	lake
جبل	[jabal]	mountain
صحراء	[ṣaḥrā’]	desert
مطر	[maṭar]	rain
شجرة	[šajara]	tree
زهرة	[zahra]	flower
شمس	[šams]	sun
قمر	[qamar]	moon
ريح	[rīḥ]	wind
سماء	[samā’]	sky
نار	[nār]	fire
جليد	[jalīd]	ice

ADJECTIVES

كبير	[kabīr]	big
صغير	[ṣaghīr]	small
طيب	[ṭayyib]	good
سيئ	[sayyi’]	bad
حار	[ḥārr]	hot
بارد	[bārid]	cold
رخيص	[rakhīṣ]	cheap
غال	[ghālin]	expensive
سعيد	[saعīd]	happy
حزين	[ḥazīn]	sad

NUMBERS

واحد	[wāḥid]	one
اثنان	[ithnān]	two
ثلاثة	[thalātha]	three
أربعة	['arbaɛa]	four
خمسة	[khamsa]	five
ستة	[sitta]	six
سبعة	[sabɛa]	seven
ثمانية	[thamāniya]	eight
تسعة	[tisɛa]	nine
عشرة	[ɛašara]	ten

TIME

يوم	[yawm]	day
شهر	[šahr]	month
عام	[ɛām]	year
ساعة	[sāɛa]	hour
اليوم	[al-yawm]	today
غدا	[ghadan]	tomorrow
أمس	['ams]	yesterday

DAYS OF THE WEEK

الأحد	[al-'aḥad]	Sunday
الاثنين	[al-ithnayn]	Monday
الثلاثاء	[ath-thulāthā']	Tuesday
الأربعاء	[al-'arbaɛā']	Wednesday
الخميس	[al-khamīs]	Thursday
الجمعة	[al-jumɛa]	Friday
السبت	[as-sabt]	Saturday

MONTHS (GREGORIAN)

يناير	[yanāyīr]	January
فبراير	[fibrāyīr]	February
مارس	[mars]	March
أبريل	[’abrīl]	April
مايو	[māyū]	May
يونيو	[yūniyō]	June
يوليو	[yūliyō]	July
أغسطس	[’aghusṭus]	August
سبتمبر	[sibtimbir]	September
أكتوبر	[’oktōbir]	October
نوفمبر	[nūfimbir]	November
دسمبر	[disembir]	December

MONTHS (ISLAMIC)

محرم	[muḥarram]	Muharram
صفر	[ṣafar]	Safar
ربيع الأول	[rabīع al-’awwal]	Rabia I
ربيع الآخر	[rabīع al-’ākhir]	Rabia II
جمادى الأولى	[jumādā l-’ūlā]	Jumada I
جمادى الآخرة	[jumādā l-’ākhira]	Jumada II
رجب	[rajab]	Rajab
شعبان	[šaعbān]	Sha’aban
رمضان	[ramaḍān]	Ramadan
شوال	[šawwāl]	Shawwal
ذو القعدة	[dhū l-qaعda]	Dhu al-Qi'dah
ذو الحجة	[dhū l-ḥijja]	Dhul Hijjah

PROPER NAMES

عرب	[ʿarab]	Arab
عربي	[ʿarabī]	Arabic
إسلام	['islām]	Islam
مسلم	[muslim]	Muslim
مصر	[miṣr]	Egypt
القاهرة	[al-qāhira]	Cairo
الأردن	[al-'urdunn]	Jordan
سوريا	[sūriyā]	Syria
لبنان	[lubnān]	Lebanon
أبو ظبي	['abū ẓabī]	Abu Dhabi
قطر	[qaṭar]	Qatar

GLOSSARY – ALPHABETICAL ORDER

– ا –

أب	['ab]	father
أبريل	['abrīl]	April
أبو ظبي	['abū ẓabī]	Abu Dhabi
أبيض	['abyaḍ]	white
أحمر	['aḥmar]	red
أخ	['akh]	brother
أخت	['ukht]	sister
أخضر	['akhḍar]	green
أذن	['udhun]	ear
أربعة	['arbaƐa]	four
أزرق	['azraq]	blue
أسود	['aswad]	black
أصفر	['aṣfar]	yellow
أغسطس	['aghusṭus]	August
أكتوبر	['oktōbir]	October
أم	['umm]	mother
أمس	['ams]	yesterday
أنف	['anf]	nose
إسلام	['islām]	Islam
إنسان	['insān]	person
ابن	[ibn]	son
اثنان	[ithnān]	two
الأحد	[al-'aḥad]	Sunday
الأربعاء	[al-'arbaƐā']	Wednesday
الأردن	[al-'urdunn]	Jordan
الاثنين	[al-ithnayn]	Monday
الثلاثاء	[ath-thulāthā']	Tuesday
الجمعة	[al-jumƐa]	Friday
الخميس	[al-khamīs]	Thursday

السبت	[as-sabt]	Saturday
القاهرة	[al-qāhira]	Cairo
اليوم	[al-yawm]	today
امرأة	[imra'a]	woman

– ب –

باب	[bāb]	door
بارد	[bārid]	cold
باص	[bāṣ]	bus
بحر	[baḥr]	sea
بحيرة	[buḥayra]	lake
بدن	[badan]	body
بقرة	[baqara]	cow
بلد	[balad]	country (state)
بنت	[bint]	daughter / girl
بنطلون	[banṭalūn]	pants
بنك	[bank]	bank
بيت	[bayt]	house
بيرة	[bīra]	beer

– ت –

تسعة	[tisعa]	nine
تفاحة	[tuffāḥa]	apple

– ث –

ثلاثة	[thalātha]	three
ثمانية	[thamāniya]	eight

– ج –

جامعة	[jāmiعa]	university
جبل	[jabal]	mountain
جبن	[jubn]	cheese
جليد	[jalīd]	ice
جمادى الآخرة	[jumādā l-'ākhira]	6th month (Islamic)
جمادى الأولى	[jumādā l-'ūlā]	5th month (Islamic)
جمل	[jamal]	camel

– ح –

حار	[ḥārr]	hot
حديقة	[ḥadīqa]	park
حذاء	[ḥidhā']	shoe
حزين	[ḥazīn]	sad
حصان	[ḥiṣān]	horse
حليب	[ḥalīb]	milk
حيوان	[ḥayawān]	animal

– خ –

خبز	[khubz]	bread
خمسة	[khamsa]	five

– د –

دراجة	[darrāja]	bicycle
دسمبر	[disembir]	December
دكان	[dukkān]	store / shop
دم	[dam]	blood

– ذ –

ذراع	[dhirāع]	arm
ذو الحجة	[dhū l-ḥijja]	12th month (Islam.)
ذو القعدة	[dhū l-qaعda]	11th month (Islam.)

– ر –

رأس	[ra's]	head
ربيع الآخر	[rabīع al-'ākhir]	4th month (Islamic)
ربيع الأول	[rabīع al-'awwal]	3rd month (Islamic)
رجب	[rajab]	7th month (Islamic)
رجل	[rajul]	man
رجل	[rijl]	leg / foot
رخيص	[rakhīṣ]	cheap
رضيع	[raḍīع]	baby
رمضان	[ramaḍān]	Ramadan
ريح	[rīḥ]	wind

– ز –

زهرة	[zahra]	flower

– س –

ساعة	[sāعa]	hour
سبتمبر	[sibtimbir]	September
سبعة	[sabعa]	seven
ستة	[sitta]	six
سعيد	[saعīd]	happy
سماء	[samā’]	sky
سمكة	[samaka]	fish
سوريا	[sūriyā]	Syria
سوق	[sūq]	market
سيئ	[sayyi’]	bad
سيارة	[sayyāra]	car (automobile)

– ش –

شارع	[šāriع]	street
شاي	[šāy]	tea
شجرة	[šajara]	tree
شعبان	[šaعbān]	8th month (Islamic)
شعر	[šaعr]	hair
شمس	[šams]	sun
شهر	[šahr]	month
شوال	[šawwāl]	Shawwal

– ص –

صحراء	[ṣaḥrā’]	desert
صديق	[ṣadīq]	friend
صغير	[ṣaghīr]	small
صفر	[ṣafar]	Safar

– ط –

طائر	[ṭā’ir]	bird
طائرة	[ṭā’ira]	airplane
طاولة	[ṭāwila]	table
طعام	[ṭaع ām]	food
طفل	[ṭifl]	child
طيب	[ṭayyib]	good

– ع –

عام	[ع ām]	year
عرب	[ع arab]	Arab
عربي	[ع arabī]	Arabic
عشاء	[ع ašā’]	dinner
عشرة	[ع ašara]	ten
عصير	[ع aṣīr]	juice
عظم	[ع aẓm]	bone
عين	[ع ayn]	eye

– غ –

غال	[ghālin]	expensive
غدا	[ghadan]	tomorrow
غداء	[ghadā’]	lunch

– ف –

فأرة	[fa’ra]	mouse
فبراير	[fibrāyīr]	February
فطور	[fuṭūr]	breakfast

فم	[fam]	mouth
فندق	[funduq]	hotel

– ق –

قارب	[qārib]	boat
قبعة	[qubbaعa]	hat
قط	[qiṭṭ]	cat
قطار	[qiṭār]	train
قطر	[qaṭar]	Qatar
قمر	[qamar]	moon
قميص	[qamīṣ]	shirt
قهوة	[qahwa]	coffee

– ك –

كبير	[kabīr]	big
كتاب	[kitāb]	book
كرسي	[kursī]	chair
كلب	[kalb]	dog
كنيسة	[kanīsa]	church

– ل –

لا	[lā]	no
لبنان	[lubnān]	Lebanon
لحم	[laḥm]	meat
لحية	[liḥya]	beard
لون	[lawn]	color

— م —

ماء	[mā’]	water
مارس	[mars]	March
مايو	[māyū]	May
محرم	[muḥarram]	Muharram
مدرسة	[madrasa]	school
مدينة	[madīna]	city
مستشفى	[mustašfa]	hospital
مسجد	[masjid]	mosque
مسلم	[muslim]	Muslim
مصر	[miṣr]	Egypt
مطار	[maṭār]	airport
مطر	[maṭar]	rain
مطعم	[maṭعam]	restaurant
ملابس	[malābis]	clothing

— ن —

نار	[nār]	fire
نافذة	[nāfidha]	window
نعم	[naعam]	yes
نهر	[nahr]	river
نوفمبر	[nūfimbir]	November

— و —

واحد	[wāḥid]	one
وجه	[wajh]	face
ولد	[walad]	boy

– ى –

يد	[yad]	hand
يناير	[yanāyīr]	January
يوليو	[yūliyō]	July
يوم	[yawm]	day
يونيو	[yūniyō]	June

Made in the USA
Columbia, SC
18 November 2022

71586067R00035